contents

We Can Work it Out
Parenting with confidence

Introduction

"Children should be seen and not heard" is as old-fashioned a term in modern parenting as "spare the rod and spoil the child".

Encouraging young children to discuss, negotiate, listen and consider others' opinions sets in place skills that are vital to their future formal education and relationships. Parents, too, need to discuss, negotiate, listen to and consider their children's views, if children are to learn these skills. Parents are the first and most important role models for young children.

Teaching children self-discipline and helping them to understand where the boundaries for behaviour lie is a responsibility that all parents have. Parents are not always with their children 24 hours a day. Yet we know that children are not always 'little angels'. Sometimes it is a struggle to deal with children's challenging behaviour in a way that teaches children the importance of those boundaries.

Smacking

Save the Children, along with the majority of child health, care and welfare organisations, believes that it is not acceptable to smack children. Experience has shown that other methods of managing children's behaviour have been found to be successful without the need for adults to resort to physical or emotional punishment.

Save the Children believes that smacking is harmful to children and to parents, does not work, and teaches children that hitting others smaller than themselves is OK. We believe that parents should be supported to find other methods of managing children's behaviour.

The United Nations Convention on the Rights of the Child (1989)

This Convention is about protecting the human dignity of the child. It requires States to protect children from all forms of physical or mental violence, injury or abuse, neglect or maltreatment (Article 19). The UK Government signed up to the Convention in 1990. Yet the reality for children in the UK is that beating, slapping and smacking remains widespread and prevalent. Physical punishment is a form of violation of the human dignity of the child. Save the Children works with parents and other agencies to campaign to protect children from all forms of violence.

The law

The use of excessive force or the occurrence of accidental injuries leaves a child in real danger of abuse or maltreatment, and the parent in real danger of accusations of assault. Today in the UK the use of 'reasonable' force on a child is accepted as a defence in law, and yet it is illegal for one adult to assault another adult. Save the Children believes that children should have the same protection in law as adults, and that changes to the law should be accompanied by a national information, awareness-raising and education programme to support parents in finding other methods of managing children's behaviour.

Countries such as Sweden, Finland, Denmark, Austria and Norway have already outlawed the physical punishment of children, combining this with positive parenting education programmes.

Foreword

" ... I wouldn't smack any of my children anyway because they will just start smacking other people and if I smack someone, then they are going to start smacking other people, because they think grown-ups do it; and if the law didn't allow smacking, I would just send them out to their room and let them have a think about it." These are the words of a seven-year-old girl.

Powerful words that show a deep understanding at an early age of why smacking does not work – confirming how it teaches children to hit others and continue the cycle of violence. This child has already begun to think about alternatives to smacking should the law be changed – a lesson to us all.

As a children's charity, Save the Children listens and responds to children like these. Our aim is to build a better world for children, and that often requires a radical change in how children are treated. We work with children and adults across the world in making these changes.

We hope this pack will enable parents and carers to discuss, consider, and learn new ways of dealing with children's behaviour. Ways which respect children's human rights to their physical and emotional integrity, and benefit families and society as a whole.

Mike Aaronson
Director General
Save the Children

This pack reflects the philosophy of the Liverpool Parent School Partnership which recognises that parents are not only the first educators of their own children, but also the first and most important role models for their children.

The collaboration between the Liverpool Parent School Partnership and Save the Children ensured that parents were able to contribute their skills, knowledge and expertise to the development of the materials in this pack. I am sure that this valuable input from parents will help to make this pack a welcome and well-used resource for parent groups and those who work with parents.

The pack promotes a sensitive, caring and holistic approach to managing children's challenging behaviour. It provides parents with a wide range of practical ideas and tips, including a very useful section on healthy living.

Being a parent is one of the most valuable, rewarding and fulfilling roles in life. However, it can also be very demanding and challenging. I am confident that this pack will support parents in fulfilling their roles and meeting these challenges.

Teresa Cassidy
Outreach Worker
Liverpool Parent School
Partnership

The package

There are many titles for those who may have the responsibility of 'parenting' children today: parents, grandparents, foster parents, adoptive parents, carers, etc. This publication can be used with all these groups, but for simplicity, the term 'parents' will be used throughout to describe the wide range.

We Can Work it Out is a support package for parent groups and those who work with parents. This training pack provides materials for a half-day workshop, helping parents reflect on how they could manage their children's challenging behaviour without resorting to emotional or physical punishment. It helps parents, in a supportive environ-ment, to consider what behaviour they find challenging; how adults respond when angry; what children see happening; and how children learn challenging behaviour from adults. It goes on to offer advice in helping children focus on requests from parents, and how to help young children understand and improve their behaviour. Accompanying this training pack is a parent booklet for parents to take home, which offers further tips and advice on behaviour management techniques.

Aims of the workshop

1. To identify methods of dealing with challenging behaviour without the use of physical or emotional punishment.

2. To reinforce and promote positive behaviour in children.

3. To gain an understanding of the rights and needs of children to grow up in a non-violent home.

4. To gain an understanding of the rights and needs of parents to live in harmony with their children.

The workshop will be useful for anyone intending to study for National Vocational Qualifications (NVQs) in Child Care and Education. It contributes to the development of the background knowledge and understanding necessary for the units on managing children's behaviour.

The *We Can Work it Out* materials were produced following discussions and piloting of the session with Liverpool parents, and work carried out by the Parent Advice Centre, Belfast. Save the Children has also produced training materials for those who work with other people's children, e.g. nursery workers and childminders, called *Let's Work Together: Managing Children's Behaviour.*

Good parenting is not instinctive. It is not always an easy task. We learn the art from those who raised us as children, and from the practices we witness across society in general.

We Can Work it Out and *Let's Work Together* are a contribution to supporting that most valuable and important role in society – parenting.

Using this pack

Section a: provides guidance for tutors to enable them to work through the pack with a group of parents/carers.

Section b: provides a pack suitable for photocopying. A complete copy of section b should be given to each parent at the beginning of the session for their personal use, and to take home with them.

Section c: gives information on further reading materials and resources, with additional materials to photocopy as hand-outs for parents.

Tutor tips

This workshop is suitable for a group of parents and/or carers no larger than 20, dividing into small groups of five or six.

The workshop is designed to last two-and-a-half hours, with a short comfort break. Activity times are flexible and for guidance only. However, timing is important for completing the process of moving from considering challenging behaviour to reinforcing positive behaviour in children.

It is essential that you work through all of the materials. It is more productive for parents if they are able to attend the complete session.

You will hear parents use a variety of terms for challenging and acceptable behaviour, e.g. good, bad, naughty. Point out to parents that for the purpose of this workshop all descriptions will be accepted, as these are terms that people use and are comfortable with when describing their feelings. However, make it clear that these are descriptions of behaviour, not descriptions of the child; we are not labelling children but separating the behaviour from the child.

Be sensitive to people who are reluctant to write things down, whether it is because they are not using their mother tongue or they just don't feel comfortable about writing. Participants will be working in groups and will be able to opt out of writing if they wish.

Additional reading materials and resources should be distributed at the end of the session.

This is a very visual workshop, where the impact of the collated responses is very effective. Display all flipchart work on the wall as each sheet is completed.

Don't forget the Attendance Certificates to acknowledge their hard work!

Tutor tools

Flipchart, marker pens, Blu-tack.

section a
tutor pack

Aims of the session

1

To identify methods of dealing with challenging behaviour without the use of physical or emotional punishment.

2

To reinforce and promote positive behaviour in children.

3

To gain an understanding of the rights and needs of children to grow up in a non-violent home.

4

To gain an understanding of the rights and needs of parents to live in harmony with their children.

We Can Work it Out
Parenting with confidence

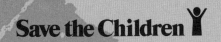

Workshop programme

Ground rules

How do adults react to challenging behaviour in a negative way?

Acceptable behaviour

How can parents help children to learn to behave well?

Let's communicate!

Why won't she do as I ask?

Giving praise

Finish and homework

Ground rules for tutors and participants

Being a parent is possibly one of the toughest jobs there is, and yet it is also one of the most rewarding. Feeling confident about the good job they do in raising children from babies to adults is a major step if parents are to have a happy and healthy relationship with their children. It is important therefore, that responses to comments from participants should be supportive, non-judgemental, understanding and tactful.

You may find during the session that discussing behaviour management raises strong feelings as individuals recall their own childhood. For some these will be memories of happy experiences, for others the memories may be distressful. The experiences they have had may also be influencing the way they are parenting and managing the behaviour of their own children. The workshop may challenge parents' firmly held views developed from their own childhood experiences, cultural or social practice.

You need to consider how you would respond to comments such as: "I used to wet the bed in fear of my mother" or "My father smacked me on a regular basis and it never did me any harm". The question should be put: "Does this mean that hitting children is OK?" Research[1] into children's views of smacking suggests that most children define smacking as hitting, with many children saying that they were themselves smacked for hitting or hurting others.

Activity time: 5 minutes

The following are basic ground rules that should be agreed and observed by the group. You need to discuss with the group at this point your position on any child protection concerns that are raised. You could ask participants if they have any other ground rules they would like included in the following:

● Respect confidentiality

● Respect each other's feelings

● Value all that is said

● Challenge discriminatory statements in a positive way

● Listen to each other and let everyone have their say.

---

1. *It Hurts You Inside: Children talking about smacking* by Carolyne Willow and Tina Hyder, published by the National Children's Bureau in association with Save the Children.

Ice-breaking exercise

Activity time: 10 minutes

Participants work in pairs, preferably with someone they don't know, introducing themselves to each other for about two minutes each.

Name

Names and ages of any children

Describe something positive that has happened to you this week

Everyone gets back together in the large group. Each of the pair introduces his or her partner to the rest of the group.

Challenging behaviour

Tutor tips

You will find that the flipchart sheet fills quickly. If the group needs prompting, remind them of classic 'trigger points' during the day when things can become fraught, e.g.

Mealtimes

Bedtime

Getting ready to go out

This activity sets the scene for identifying and describing clearly the behaviour of the child.

Get behind words such as 'attention seeking' or 'sulking'. These are judgements of children made by adults.

This activity aims to separate the behaviour from the child by questioning why the child is 'attention seeking' or 'sulking'.

Activity time: 5 minutes (large group)

Invite participants to call out what they feel is challenging behaviour in children.

Record everything on a flipchart (except discriminatory remarks which should be discussed).

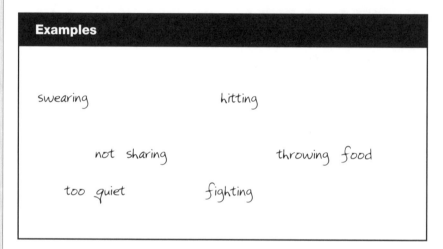

Examples

swearing   hitting

not sharing   throwing food

too quiet   fighting

Ask participants if there is anything listed that would be unacceptable at six years old, but is OK at 18 months old. Do we expect different behaviour for boys and girls?

How do adults react to challenging behaviour in a negative way?

Tutor tips

Encourage the parents to 'let their hair down'. There may be some reticence if people feel guilty about their negative behaviour. Remind them that most parents will have been in exactly the same situation!

Parents may say things they regret and try to disown, such as: "I'll strangle him." You can, with humour, record it as it can be a valuable learning point. Discuss the impact on children's self-esteem of parents' teasing, smacking, laughing at their efforts or not listening.

Body language should identify the physical stance of adults in a powerful way. Discuss this.

As a large group, compare the responses on the flip chart to the challenging behaviour recorded earlier (see page 12). It is important to discuss the impact of the adults' behaviour on children and how children observe and learn behaviour from them.

Activity time: 10 minutes (small groups)

15 minutes report back

Ask participants to turn to the first activity in their pack.

In your small group consider how adults respond, in a negative way, to challenging behaviour from children.

Think about what you see and hear in the street or supermarket and consider how adults behave when angry.

Put yourself in the child's position. What do they see, hear and have done to them when adults react to their behaviour in a negative way?

Record all the responses from your small group on your chart.

Here is an example:

Statements	Body language	Actions
"Shut up"	Hands on hips	Smacking

For your eyes only

How do we react to challenging behaviour when under pressure?
On your own, think about a child's behaviour that you may have dealt with in a negative way. Record it, just for yourself.

Acceptable behaviour

Ask the group to turn to the next page.

Individuals should work on their own, without conferring. They should identify the child's behaviour or actions, not the parent's interpretation of the situation, e.g. 'sharing toys' is the behaviour, 'being happy' is not.
Consider:
Was this an easy list to complete? (You may find that the majority found it difficult.)

Do we 'catch' children behaving badly, or 'catch' children behaving well?

Do our own personal circumstances at the time affect our responses, e.g. telephone bill arriving, late getting up in the morning?

So far, we have concentrated on challenging behaviour in children. This in itself can make us feel low. Likewise it can be difficult for parents and children to feel positive or notice positive behaviour if it's been a trying day.

Remind the parents, if appropriate, of the difficulty they had during the ice-breaker at the beginning of the session in thinking of something positive that happened to them in the last week. Point out the difference in length between the 'challenging behaviour' list and the 'acceptable behaviour' list.

Look at it from the child's point of view – how hard do they have to work to get parents to *show* how pleased they are?

Activity time: 5 minutes (individuals)

10 minutes report back

On your own list the acceptable behaviour that you would like to see in your child. Say what they will be doing.

1.

2.

3.

4.

5.

6.

For your eyes only. Activity time: 5 minutes (individuals)

How do we react to acceptable, or 'good' behaviour, during our busy day?

Record, **on your own**, your usual response.

How can parents help children to learn to behave well?

Activity time: **15 minutes (small groups)**
                           15 minutes report back

Tutor tips

This is a good activity for making parents feel more positive!

Record on the flipchart each group's response.

This activity gives the opportunity for parents to think carefully about what they say, what they can do and what they should show in their body language which will make a child realise that they have done well.

If children are to learn what behaviour is acceptable, completing the sentence will teach them. Ensure that the group completes the sentences in the 'statement' column. For example:

"Well done, Errol, for setting the table."
"Thank you, Jyotsna, for tidying the toys away."
"Hurray, Jack, you've done up your shoelaces."

Discuss with parents how this reinforces positive behaviour by helping children to fully understand what the behaviour is that has caused such praise. If parents focus on noticing acceptable behaviour, and reinforce it by the method above, children will enjoy this attention, learn how to behave well, and be less inclined to behave badly.

Ask participants to turn to the next page.

In your small group, think about how we can notice and respond to children's acceptable behaviour in a positive way. List all your group's responses on your sheet.

An example has been given:

Statements	Body language	Actions
"Well done, Laura, for sharing your toys with Simon."	Smile	Cuddle

If you give me a cuddle— I'll do the washing-up again tomorrow!

Let's communicate!

You can use these three pages 'Let's communicate!', 'Why won't she do as I ask?' and 'Giving praise' as a prompt for discussion via hand-outs, an overhead projector or a flipchart, with everyone together in the large group.

Most parents can recall their children (or they themselves when young) being given a list of tasks, e.g. "I want you to go upstairs to your room, put on your clean pyjamas that are in your drawer, then go into the bathroom and clean your teeth, tell Matthew that he is to turn down that music, and bring down your black shoes so that I can clean them... Oh, and on your way upstairs can you tell your Dad that his tea is on the table and it's getting cold?"

Is it any wonder that sometimes, at the end of a tiring day, children forget what they have been asked to do? Help children to succeed in being able to remember and complete tasks, by making your requests short and to the point.

You will find discussion points on 'punishment' and 'sanctions' in section c, 'Thinking about the words we use'.

Examples of 'when' and 'then' requests:
"When you clean your teeth I will read you a story."
"When you tidy away that jigsaw you can watch your favourite television programme."

Activity time: 10 minutes

- Make requests to your child short and to the point

- Make one request at a time

- Let your child know clearly what you would like him/her to do

- Be realistic in your expectations considering the child's age and ability

- Use 'do' rather than 'don't' requests

- Make requests polite

- Don't threaten later punishment – when Dad gets home..., etc.

- Use 'when' and 'then' requests

Why won't she do as I ask?

Life for young children today is usually busy, active, exciting, stimulating, noisy, demanding, tiring and, hopefully, fun! We all know the frustration parents feel when children are not concentrating on what parents are saying, or appear to be defiantly not listening. Children may be so wrapped up in the activity they are doing, whether it be painting, playing or watching television, that they can seem to ignore parents. The expectations that adults have of children need to be made very clear to children, according to their stage of development and ability to understand what they are being told. Parents have the same right to be heard as children do.

The suggestions listed here may go some way towards helping in those difficult times. However, if everything has been tried with no success, then listen carefully to the argument your child is putting forward. Negotiate. Try to reach a compromise. Consider whether you can accept their proposal. Does it really matter at this particular moment if your child 'wins' the argument, if it helps prevent World War Three breaking out in your home?

An example of consequences of non co-operation is: "If you don't eat your food, you will be hungry."

Activity time: 10 minutes

If your child has got into the habit of not paying attention to your requests:

● Kneel or sit so you are at her/his level

● Hold your child gently by the shoulders or hands, while you make the request

● Look right into her/his eyes

● Talk in a clear and firm voice

● Let your face look serious while you speak

● Where possible, have someone else to back you up if the child ignores you

● Make it clear that you expect to be listened to – as you would listen to them

● Listen to your child's response and carefully consider their views

● Give your child options whenever possible

● Try negotiation

● Give ample opportunity for her/him to complete the task

● Praise co-operation OR explain the consequences for non co-operation (not threats)

● Give warnings and helpful reminders, e.g. "If you continue..."

● Support your partner, and have your partner support you

● Encourage problem-solving with your child.

Are you ready to reach a compromise yet?

Giving praise

Tutor tips

During this workshop we have looked carefully at how adults often notice and give more attention to children who are not behaving well than to those who are behaving well. Discuss why this might be so and what the pressures are that can cause this to happen, e.g. fear that our children will be 'out of control'? Old views, still around, that children should be 'seen and not heard'? Busy lifestyles and packed diaries that cause difficulties when children aren't able to keep up?

Some people can be embarrassed when giving or receiving praise if they are not used to being praised themselves. Parents' own self-esteem and self-worth can contribute to their ability to recognise their own child's abilities and praise consistently and frequently. This in turn raises a child's feelings of self-worth and self-esteem. Children glow with pride when given praise, will remember it and work to achieve it again. We all need to feel good about ourselves.

Activity time: 10 minutes

- Make the praise relevant to the behaviour

- Praise immediately

- Give specific praise to help the child understand her/his behaviour (complete the sentence)

- Give positive praise without qualifiers or sarcasm

- Praise with smiles, eye contact and enthusiasm, as well as with words

- Give pats, hugs and kisses along with verbal praise

- 'Catch' your child when s/he is behaving well – don't save praise for perfect behaviour only

- Use praise consistently whenever you see the positive behaviour you want to encourage

- Praise in front of other people

- Increase praise for difficult children

- Show the child how to praise her/himself for appropriate behaviour

- Reward your child with a treat for behaving well, e.g. choosing a trip out (try to avoid sweets)

- Do not offer your child a treat in the form of a bribe to stop them behaving badly (spoiling the child)

Finish

Tutor tips

Reassure the parents that it's tough trying to ignore challenging behaviour, hence the homework lasting for just two weeks!

Practice shows that two weeks of concentrated effort can become a habit, and parents will find that it becomes easier to focus on the positive as time goes by. Parents should also find that it will influence change for the better in their children's behaviour, and makes life less stressful for everyone.

Activity time: 10 minutes

Take time to distribute handouts, evaluation sheets and attendance certificates.

Homework

Ask the parents to try and ignore their children's challenging behaviour for the next two weeks and concentrate on noticing and reinforcing the positive behaviour, unless the challenging behaviour:

● is dangerous or hurtful to someone else

● is dangerous to the child

● will make the child unwelcome or unacceptable to other people

● damages other people's property.

section b
student pack

Aims of the session

1

To identify methods of dealing with challenging behaviour without the use of physical or emotional punishment.

2

To reinforce and promote positive behaviour in children.

3

To gain an understanding of the rights and needs of children to grow up in a non-violent home.

4

To gain an understanding of the rights and needs of parents to live in harmony with their children.

We Can Work it Out
Parenting with confidence

Workshop programme

Ground rules

How do adults react to challenging behaviour in a negative way?

Acceptable behaviour

How can parents help children to learn to behave well?

Let's communicate!

Why won't she do as I ask?

Giving praise

Ground rules

● Respect confidentiality

● Respect each other's feelings

● Value all that is said

● Challenge discriminatory statements in a positive way

● Listen to each other and let everyone have their say

How do adults react to challenging behaviour in a negative way?

In your small group consider how adults respond, in a negative way, to challenging behaviour from children. Think about what you see and hear in the street or supermarket and consider how adults behave when angry. Put yourself in the child's position. What do they see, hear and have done to them when adults react to their behaviour in a negative way? You could get one of your group to role-play 'anger' and record on the chart what you see.

One example has been given. List as many as you can think of:

Statements	Body Language	Actions
"Shut up."	Smacking	Hands on hips

For your eyes only

How do we react to challenging behaviour when under pressure?
On your own, think about a child's behaviour that you may have dealt with in a negative way. Record it, just for yourself.

Acceptable behaviour

We found it fairly easy to identify challenging behaviour. Now we are going to look at 'acceptable' behaviour.

On your own list the acceptable behaviour that you would like to see in your child.

Say what they will be doing.

1.

2.

3.

4.

5.

6.

For your eyes only

How do we react to acceptable, or 'good' behaviour, during our busy day?
Record here, **on your own**, your usual response.

How can parents help children to learn to behave well?

In your small group, think about how we can notice and respond to children's acceptable behaviour in a positive way. Think about what you can say and do and the visual expressions which can reinforce positive behaviour in children.

List all your group's responses on your chart.

An example has been given:

Statements	Body language	Actions
"Well done, Laura, for sharing your toys with Simon."	Smile	Cuddle

If you give me a cuddle — I'll do the washing-up again tomorrow!

Let's communicate!

- Make requests to your child short and to the point

- Make one request at a time

- Let your child know clearly what you would like her/him to do

- Be realistic in your expectations considering the child's age and ability

- Use 'do' rather than 'don't' requests

- Make requests polite

- Don't threaten later punishment – when Dad gets home…, etc.

- Use 'when' and 'then' requests

Notes:

Why won't she do as I ask?

If your child has got into the habit of not paying attention to your requests:

- Kneel or sit so you are at his/her level

- Hold your child gently by the shoulders or hands, while you make the request

- Look right into her/his eyes

- Talk in a clear and firm voice

- Let your face look serious while you speak

- Where possible, have someone else to back you up if the child ignores you

- Make it clear that you expect to be listened to – as you would listen to them

- Listen to your child's response and carefully consider their views

- Give your child options whenever possible

- Try negotiation

- Give ample opportunity for her/him to complete the task

- Praise co-operation OR explain the consequences for non co-operation (not threats)

- Give warnings and helpful reminders, e.g. "If you continue..."

- Support your partner, and have your partner support you

- Encourage problem-solving with your child.

Notes:

Are you ready to reach a compromise yet?

Giving praise

- Make the praise relevant to the behaviour

- Praise immediately

- Give specific praise to help the child understand her/his behaviour (complete the sentence)

- Give positive praise without qualifiers or sarcasm

- Praise with smiles, eye contact and enthusiasm, as well as with words

- Give pats, hugs and kisses along with verbal praise

- 'Catch' your child when s/he is behaving well – don't save praise for perfect behaviour only

- Use praise consistently whenever you see the positive behaviour you want to encourage

- Praise in front of other people

- Increase praise for difficult children

- Show the child how to praise her/himself for appropriate behaviour

- Reward your child with a treat for behaving well, e.g. choosing a trip out (try to avoid sweets)

- Do not offer your child a treat in the form of a bribe to stop behaving badly (spoiling the child)

Notes:

section c
further reading and resources

We Can Work it Out

Parenting with confidence

Save the Children

Ten Tactics for Positive Parenting

1 Make sure that the environment you are in, or your home, is 'child friendly', with danger and temptation out of the way of the children!

7 Use a variety of ways to reinforce acceptable behaviour, e.g. display children's paintings.

2 Make sure that the children know what they are doing and what is expected of them.

5 Try to praise quickly and consistently, and let others know when they have done well.

8 Make sure your child knows exactly what behaviour she or he is being praised for by completing the sentence, e.g. "Well done, Jack, you've tied up your shoe laces!"

3 Help them to make and keep a few simple, positive rules, e.g. "In our home we share our toys."

9 Always let your child know that you love them and still like them, no matter what their behaviour!

6 As far as possible ignore 'bad' behaviour (try not to nag).

4 Concentrate on noticing the 'good' behaviour or work in your child (catch them being 'good').

10 Build treats into your day as rewards for especially 'good' behaviour (try to avoid sweets).

Thinking about the words we use

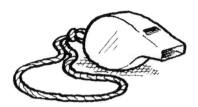

Discipline

Some people might understand this to mean punishment, especially corporal or physical punishment, but it's really about giving children guidance about how to behave in ways which will not harm other people or themselves. Discipline can be firm, without adults resorting to physical hurt to children. All children need to learn self-discipline as they grow and develop, so that they can learn to control their own behaviour.

Rules

Does this make you think of school rules? We could think of setting positive house rules: "In this house we share our toys"; "In this house we say please and thank you". A few, very clear rules can help children avoid behaviour which will harm and upset other people. Most children want to please their parents and receive praise for doing well, so rules expressed in positive ways – saying what is acceptable – are more helpful than a list of 'don'ts'.

Limits, boundaries

These words may feel less harsh than rules. Children certainly do benefit from parents making clear to them where the boundaries for behaviour lie. When they know that there are certain limits beyond which they are not permitted to go, children usually feel more secure and relaxed, in the knowledge of what behaviour is acceptable.

Expectations

This is a positive way of talking about behaviour since it actually describes what parents expect of children, what we do want them to do, and gives them something to live up to. Expectations about behaviour must be made very clear to children, according to their stage of development and ability to understand what they are being told. Children who live up to the expectations set for them deserve praise.

Unacceptable behaviour

This phrase always leaves the question dangling – unacceptable to whom, and why? Rules, limits, boundaries and expectations should all be set according to whether certain behaviour will or will not harm other people (physically or their feelings), damage other people's possessions, or just make the child concerned unwelcome in their community. While we may not want our children to be forced to conform to rigid sets of rules and manners based on unreasonably authoritarian codes, we do all know that some ways of behaving just cannot be tolerated in society, and our children need to start learning about this very young – for their own sakes in later life.

Uncontrollable

In what ways do we really think we can or should 'control' children, and

to what extent? Setting out to control a child is an unwinnable battle. In any case, children are human beings with rights which adults should respect. An important part of growing up is about developing self-control so that children are able to manage their strong feelings, like frustration and anger, in ways which avoid damaging other people or infringing their rights as human beings. Parents should not be trying to control children, but help children learn how to control their own behaviour. We should talk with children about how they feel, using books and stories (perhaps with dolls and puppets), to help them express what they feel.

Problem behaviour

Again, we need to ask – a problem for whom? It's important not to let concerns about children's behaviour get out of hand so that annoying incidents are blown up out of proportion, and a child gets labelled as a 'problem'. Some behaviour which is difficult for parents to cope with has been shown to have its origins in physical ailments or even allergies. Often children behave in ways which try the patience of adults because of some disturbing or distressing event in their lives. In such a situation, children need extra attention and help to cope with the confusions, resentments or other negative feelings they are experiencing, and to find ways of channelling such feeling into ways of behaving that don't harm themselves or others.

Attention seeking

Using this term suggests that the child seeking attention is in some

way to blame, and that this is a form of behaviour to disapprove of. We have to ask ourselves why a child needs to seek attention – are they not being given attention? Focusing on a child's needs includes giving your child attention, listening to what they say, communicating with them, with eye contact and in conversation. Some-times it is necessary for one child to wait a little for attention because the needs of another child must take priority, and we must help children to learn to wait to be given attention. Children can learn to ask for help or information in acceptable ways. We shouldn't object to children seeking attention, just to the unacceptable ways they sometimes use!

Punishment

All too often parents' response to handling children's behaviour is to focus on ways of punishing them for negative behaviour, rather than on positive ways of reinforcing welcome behaviour. Punishments don't tend to be very effective. Young children have difficulty making connections between the behaviour which has given rise to the punishment and the punishment itself, especially if they are separated in time, or have no connection with one another.

Sanctions

This is a less 'heavy' way of talking about punishment. For older children, depriving them of treats and privileges may influence them to change their behaviour in future. For younger children, there must be some meaningful link between the behaviour and the sanction – for instance, clearing up something which has been thrown or dropped on purpose.

Naughty

This is a very unhelpful word to use about children. Some parents even seem to think that all children are naturally 'naughty' and go out of their way to annoy and pester adults. In fact, most children want to be 'good' so they will win the approval and affection of parents. Children's lively behaviour or early attempts to assert themselves as independent people are not being 'naughty', and neither is their fractiousness when they're tired, bored or unwell. This is a label to avoid – it might become an expectation that children will live up to!

Naughty chairs

Making a child sit on a chair, stand in a corner or against a wall in the sight of others is a form of humiliation and should never be used. It will build up your child's feelings of resentment and only make a situation more highly charged. The public stocks were abolished centuries ago! Having a quiet corner, where your child can go for 'time out' to calm down and recover in private and with dignity, is quite a different strategy.

Smacking

It is not acceptable to hit children. There is never a good reason to smack your child. It causes emotional hurt and confusion to the child as well as physical pain. All that children will learn from being smacked is that it's OK to hit others, especially if you are bigger and more powerful. This is teaching our children how to bully. Parents are not allowed by law to hit each other or other adults. Children should have the same rights to protection from physical assault as adults do.

Positive parenting, without resorting to physical punishment, is about:

- Creating a framework for children's behaviour; making our expectations very clear to our children; recognising their stage of development and ability to understand what they are being told.

- Reinforcing positive behaviour at every opportunity, with approval, praise and even rewards.

- Applying expectations and rules consistently – both from one time to another, to children of both genders, and to children of what ever racial, cultural or social background.

- Developing a range of strategies for dealing with behaviour which falls short of adults' expectations – distracting the child; removing them from the situation; explaining why something is unacceptable or why someone else has been hurt; giving the child a chance to take some 'time out' to calm down and regain control.

Healthy living

In the course of a week do you ever find yourself reacting differently to the same situation? One day you can find four-year-old Angie's attempts at tidying up the toys helpful, yet two days later your patience is wearing thin as you try to hurry her up – and she drops the paint in the rush.

Don't worry! This is usual behaviour in many adults – the day-to-day responsibilities, worries and changes in our lives can make our approach to caring for children differ so much that Angie doesn't know when she is doing things right and when she is doing things wrong.

If you can find the time, step back and consider what might be making you feel the pressure.

If the situation cannot be improved immediately, try some of these stress management techniques to relieve any tensions.

And remember, stress simply means pressure, and it happens to all of us. Recognising it goes a long way towards improving your relationship with your child, and helps you realise that they are probably doing their best.

Relaxation

Learning how to relax is very important as relaxation allows the body to rest and heal itself, both physically and psychologically. Relaxation is as important to children as it is to adults.

Tension and relaxation cannot exist together – try tensing your fist and relaxing it at the same time. The problems arise when you hold on to tension long after the need has gone, e.g. have you ever found yourself frowning, clenching your fist or teeth, and not even realised you were doing it?

Take the time to listen to what your body is saying and become aware of your own particular tension trigger points. This is the first step on the road to feeling able to deal with the stresses and strains in your life.

Breathing

Breathing is a good indicator of your anxiety state. Learning how to breathe properly will help you feel better and ease any tension.

Stand up against a wall, with your heels, shoulders and head touching the wall. This will help you with your general posture. Step away from the wall and see how this compares with your normal stance.

1. Stand with your feet under your hips, toes pointing forward. Let your spine become erect and your head balance on top. Feel your body balancing and becoming as symmetrical as possible.

2. Let your fingers rest on your stomach, fingertips touching. Take a deep breath in. Breathe out and pull your stomach in, pushing all

the air out. Now breathe in and expand your stomach; breathe out and push all the breath out. Inhale to the count of four heartbeats; exhale to the count of six. Do this seven times in the morning and whenever you have time during the day.

3. Clasp your hands behind your back. Do this gently; never stretch into pain. Take a deep breath, push your hands down and let your head fall back. Breathe out. Now breathe in.

    As you breathe out, bend forward till your spine is parallel with the floor; arms are still up. Breathe in again and come up as you breathe out.

4. Take a deep breath and hum as you breathe out. Time yourself and see if you can increase the length of the hum.

5. If your child is comfortable with this, place your hand on her/his stomach and breathe with your child, trying to get them to take longer breaths with you. You can make a game of this or do it quietly when you are reading to your child or giving them cuddle.

    If you feel any pain or discomfort, more than you would feel with a gentle stretch, stop and check with your doctor before you continue.

Exercise

The body and mind are closely inter-linked. Here are some simple, gentle exercises that will get your whole body into a state for learning. You could make this into a game with the children.

1. Starting with your toes, work up the body circling all your joints slowly three times in each direction.

2. March on the spot, touching your right hand to your left knee and your left hand to your right knee. Do this for three minutes. Now repeat, but this time touching your left hand to your left knee and your right hand to your right knee.

3. Look up at the ceiling and, keeping your nose fixed on a spot, draw an imaginary butterfly (figure of eight) with your eyes, making sure you start at the bottom and go up.

Assertiveness

Assertiveness is not aggression. It comes from a sense of quiet inner confidence that you are at all times and in all places doing the best you can. There is an ability to learn and be open to new information which helps you adapt and function more successfully in all aspects of your life.

It is the ability to say no – to state your truth quietly and with gentle strength.

It is about knowing yourself a little and owning your problems, leaving guilt trips and emotional threats to others.

Sensitivity

Many people think that, with *some* children, diet can now affect both learning and behaviour.

The main clue to sensitivity is a craving, usually for the thing you have most often, possibly the thing you like best.

Here is a list of some of the most common foods that can cause sensitivities:

1. Dairy products
2. Sugar
3. Colourings in sweets, drinks, cakes and lots of convenience foods
4. Crisps, artificial flavouring
5. Cola
6. Wheat

Does your child have any of these symptoms?

Physical
1. Asthma
2. Eczema
3. Recurring ear or throat infections
4. Clumsiness/poor co-ordination
5. Tiredness/over-activity

Emotional
1. Quick temper
2. Lack of impulse control
3. Mood swings
4. Detachment

Mental
1. Lack of concentration
2. Daydreaming
3. Forgetfulness
4. Learning disorders

What can you do about your child's diet?

- Cut down slowly on the suspected food
- Drink plenty of bottled water
- Eat fresh or dried fruit
- Cook food as little as possible if safe to do so
- Eat fresh vegetables raw
- Cut down white sugar gradually and change to raw cane
- Eat breakfast
- Eat regularly
- Avoid anything labelled 'diet'
- Cut down tea and coffee
- Try and ensure a balanced diet which includes essential vitamins and minerals
- A smoke-free environment is healthiest for your children

If your child fails to respond to any of these measures consider talking to your doctor or health visitor.

Evaluation Sheet

Workshop title _____   Date _____

What was good for you?

What was not so good?

This is to certify that

_____

has attended a workshop on

Confident Parenting
(managing children's behaviour)

Signed _____   Date _____

Taken from the Save the Children publication **We Can Work it Out:** *Parenting with confidence*

Children learn what they live

If a child lives with criticism
s/he learns to condemn.

If a child lives with hostility
s/he learns how to fight.

If a child lives with ridicule
s/he learns to be shy.

If a child lives with tolerance
s/he learns how to be patient.

If a child lives with encouragement
s/he learns confidence.

If a child lives with praise
s/he learns to appreciate.

If a child lives with fairness
s/he learns justice.

If a child lives with security
s/he learns to have faith.

If a child lives with approval
s/he learns to like her/himself.

If a child lives with acceptance and friendship
s/he learns to find love in the world.

Dorothy Law Nolte

Further reading

An Eye for an Eye Leaves Everyone Blind: Teaching young children to settle conflicts without violence – training pack and parents' guide – Sue Finch, National Early Years Network and Save the Children, 1998

Hitting People is Wrong – and children are people too, EPOCH, 1996

It Hurts you Inside: Children talking about smacking, Carolyne Willow and Tina Hyder, Save the Children and The National Children's Bureau, 1999

Let's Work Together – a training pack for early years workers to identify children's challenging behaviour and find appropriate ways of dealing with it – Kate Harper, Save the Children, 1996

Children's books
A Boy and a Bear: The Children's Relaxation Book by Lori Lite and M Hartigan, published by Speciality Press, 1996, ISBN 1 8996941076

Feelings by Aliki, published by Piper, 1989, ISBN 0330294083

Feeling Angry by Althea Braithwaite, published by A & C Black, 1997, ISBN 0713645024

Your Emotions: I Feel Angry by Brian Moses, published by Wayland, 1994, ISBN 0750214031

Some useful addresses

B.M. CRY-SIS
London WC1N 3XX
Send s.a.e. for information
Helpline: 0171 404 5011

British Agencies for Adoption and
Fostering (BAAF)
Skyline House
200 Union Street
London SE1 OLX
0171 593 2000

Childline
2nd Floor, Royal Mall Buildings
50 Studd Street
London NI 0QW
0800 1111 (helpline)

Childline in Scotland
18 Albion Street
Glasgow G1 1LH
0800 1111 (helpline)

End Physical Punishment of Children
(EPOCH)
77 Holloway Road
London N7 8JZ
0171 700 0627

Gingerbread
16-17 Clerkenwell Close
London EC1R OAA
0171 336 8184 (advice line)

National Council for
One Parent Families
255 Kentish Town Road
London NW5 2LX
0171 843 6008

National Forum on
Children & Violence
c/o 8 Wakley Street
London EC1V 7QE
0171 843 6008

National Foster Care Association
87 Blackfriar Road
London SE1 8HA
0171 620 6400

National Newpin (New Parent
Information Network)
Sutherland House
35 Sutherland Square
Walworth
London SE17 3EE
0171 703 6326

National Society for the Prevention
of Cruelty to Children (NSPCC)
National Centre
42 Curtain Road
London EC2A 3NH
0171 825 2500

Parentline
Endway House,
The Endway
Hadleigh
Essex SS7 2AN
01702 559 900 (helpline)

Save the Children
17 Grove Lane
London SE5 8RD
0171 703 5400

Stepfamily
3rd Floor
Chapel House
18 Hatton Place
London EC1N 8RU
0171 209 2464 (helpline)